thought PROVOKERS®

By Doug Rohrer

Drawings by Joe Spooner

KEY CURRICULUM PRESS
Innovators in Mathematics Education

Copyright © 1993 by Key Curriculum Press. All rights reserved.
Published by Key Curriculum Press, 1150 65th Street, Emeryville, California 94608.
editorial@keypress.com
http://www.keypress.com
Graphics by Joe Spooner.

Printed in the United States of America   17 16 15 14 13 10 9 8   02 01 00 99 98   ISBN 1-55953-065-0

Author's Note

I believe that the vast majority of puzzles are uninteresting, often because they rely upon trial and error, formal education, or simply hard work. Ideally, a question should be intrinsically provocative, its solution should be enjoyable, and its answer should be surprising. With these criteria in mind, I have selected the following "thought provokers," comprised of both originals and embellishments of classics.

I begin each of my mathematics classes with a thought provoker—not to test students but rather to instruct them. Though most are rather difficult, creative and timely hints facilitate finding of solution as well as demonstrate problem solving skills. We work as a group so that the students can learn and enjoy rather than compete and fail. I hope that you and your classes enjoy this collection of favorites, presented in three sections: problems, hints, and answers. Finally, I am indebted to Dan Bennett, Andrea Chow, Jeff Fanton, Don Helling, Dan Lane, Adam Ray, Eric Ruthroff, and my students for their suggestions and to Joe Spooner for his illustrations.

—Doug Rohrer

About the Author

Doug Rohrer spent the better part of his formative years in the Washington, D.C. area and later attended the College of William and Mary in Virginia where he majored in Mathematics. In the following five years he taught mathematics at Pinewood School in Los Altos Hills, California, beginning each lecture with the Thought Provoker of the day. He later began mathematical research into memory at the University of California in San Diego, earning his M.A. and Ph.D. in Experimental Psychology. He continues to teach and do research.

The Ant and the Crumb

A room has a floor that is 10 feet by 38 feet and a ceiling that is 20 feet high. An ant sits 1 foot above the floor in the middle of one of the small end walls and desires a crumb that is 1 foot below the ceiling in the middle of the opposite end wall. Recalling that, in any right triangle, the hypotenuse^2 = leg^2 + leg^2, the ant crawls along the shortest possible path. Incredibly, this optimal path includes both the floor and the ceiling! How far did the ant crawl?

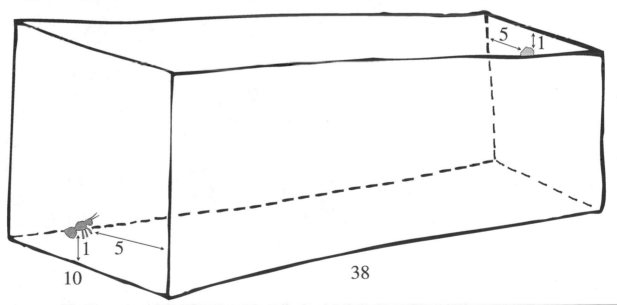

Bike Pedal

Suppose a rope is tied to the right pedal of a bike while that pedal is at its lowest point. Suppose further that the bike is balanced, the string is fully extended behind the bike, and you are facing the right side of the bike, as shown below.

1. If the rope is pulled, will the pedals rotate clockwise (as when pedaling forward) or counter-clockwise?

2. Does the bike move forward or backward, relative to the ground?

3. Does the pedal move forward or backward, relative to the ground?

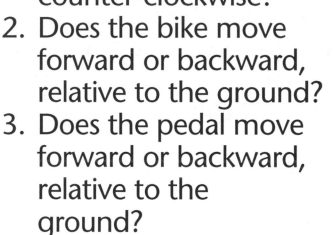

©1993 by Key Curriculum Press

Birthdays

Give an intuitive estimate of how many randomly chosen people are needed before the probability is greater than 50% that at least two of them have the same birthday?

Bloodhound

A prison guard and his bloodhound are chasing an escaped prisoner. The prisoner has a 10 mile head start but the guard is walking 1 mph faster than the prisoner. The bloodhound is trained to run to the prisoner, run back to the guard, and then continue running back and forth between them. If the bloodhound runs 10 mph, how far does the bloodhound run before the guard finally catches up to the prisoner?

Boat and Anchor

A heavy anchor is thrown from a boat. Does the water level of the lake rise, fall, or stay the same?

#5

Boys and Girls

Tanya and Bill each have two children. We know that at least one of Tanya's children is a boy and that Bill's oldest child is a boy. Explain why the probability that Tanya has two boys does NOT equal the probability that Bill has two boys.

One of mine's a boy—I haven't checked the other one yet.

Bugs on Bikes

Two bugs grow tired of walking and decide to hop onto a nearby racing bike. One bug sits within the tread of the smaller front wheel while the other bug sits within the tread of the larger back wheel. First, can you intuit the shape of the path that each bug will travel? Second, can you intuit which bug, if either, travels a greater distance through space during any given bicycle ride?

Bumpy Road

If a flexible cable is suspended between two poles (as with a cable suspension bridge), the cable forms a curve known as a catenary (from the Latin "catena," meaning chain). Suppose that a road is comprised of large arcs that are inverted catenaries, as shown in the diagram. Intuitively, can you guess what shape of tire will provide a perfectly smooth ride?

©1993 by Key Curriculum Press

Cake

How can one cut eight pieces from a round cake with three straight slices of a knife, without moving any of the pieces?

Census Taker

A census taker knocks on the door and a woman answers. She informs the census taker that she lives in the house with her three sons. The census taker asks for the ages of the boys and the woman informs him that the product of their ages equals 36 and the sum of their ages equals the address of the house next door. He finds this rather odd, but he walks to the house next door, realizes that he needs more information, and returns. He asks for another hint, and the woman tells him that only her oldest son was born in a leap year. How old are the three sons?

Chaperone

A camp counselor is hiking with Alice, Brad, and Candice. The four of them come upon a river that can only be traversed by riding a pulley chair that can hold either one or two people. Unfortunately, camp rules dictate that a counselor accompany a child on the chair. Furthermore, Brad and Candice are less than trustworthy, and the counselor does not want to leave sweet Alice alone with either of them. How do the four of them cross the river?

Counterfeit

There are twelve coins that are numbered 1 through 12. Eleven weigh the same and one is either lighter or heavier than the others. Using just three weighings with a balance scale, devise a scheme that will find the counterfeit coin AND determine whether it is lighter or heavier. (This problem is very hard.)

Crying Wolf

Name an emotion that is an anagram of a homonym of an antonym of a homonym of an anagram of *wolf*.

Cyclic Number

Find the number, *abcdef*, with non-zero, unique digits such that:

1. *fabcde* = 5 • *abcdef*
2. *efabcd* = 4 • *abcdef*
3. *defabc* = 6 • *abcdef*
4. *cdefab* = 2 • *abcdef*
5. *bcdefa* = 3 • *abcdef*

Date Dice

Office desks often have calendars in the form of blocks which can be rotated so that the date appears. How can two cubes be labeled with digits so that a surface from each combine to form every date of the month?

Dating Game

In a new version of the dating game, two of the three bachelors always lie while the other tells the truth. A woman asks questions of the men from behind a partition. She asks each man, "Which of you is the tallest?"
Bachelor 1 replies, "Not me."
Bachelor 2 replies, "I am."
Bachelor 3 replies, "Not Bachelor 2."
Who is the tallest?

Dental Dilemma

After a routine checkup and enamel test, a dentist informs Willy that he has a rare tooth condition that causes moss to grow on the teeth of 1 of every 1001 people when they reach middle age. When Willy asks about the reliability of the test, his dentist informs him that the test is extremely accurate. Only 4 out of every 1000 people who do not have the condition test falsely positive and the test never misses the presence of the condition. Willy then smiles, realizing that his odds of having the condition are quite low. What is the probability that Willy has the condition?

Dominoes

Suppose that the two squares from opposite corners of a checkerboard are removed so that only 62 squares remain. Further suppose that one has 31 dominoes, each the shape of two adjacent checkerboard squares. Prove that the 31 dominoes can NOT be arranged so that the checkerboard is completely covered.

The Earth's Equator

A string is wrapped around the Earth's equator (or circumference) and the two ends of the string just touch. Now suppose that another string is tied to the original string so that it is 100 feet longer. If this new string is placed around the equator and pulled tight so that it is suspended in air, how high will the string be above the ground.

a. Not even high enough to squeeze an atom underneath the string.

b. Just high enough to roll a bowl ing ball underneath the string.

c. Just high enough to drive a Mack truck underneath the string.

d. One hundred feet high.

Explain. Remember that, for a circle, circumference = $2\pi \cdot$ radius

Fork in the Road

A woman is walking through a town whose inhabitants either always tell the truth or always lie. She comes to a fork in the road and does not know whether the left or right road leads to her destination. What can she ask a passerby so that she can deduce the correct choice?

Four Weights

When using a balance scale, weights can be placed on either side of the scale. For example, if a 10 pound weight provides a counterbalance to an object and a 7 pound weight, then the object must weight 3 pounds. What four weights can be used to weigh objects of 1, 2, 3, ..., 38, 39, or 40 pounds?

Hmm... seems to be a rather weighty problem.

Helix

An ant climbs to the top of a soda can following a spiral path with a slope of 45°, as shown. Such a curve is called a *helix*. If the can is 6 inches tall, how far did the ant walk? The answer does not depend on the width of the can! (Remember that, for a right triangle, $leg^2 + leg^2 = hypotenuse^2$.)

This can wasn't drawn to scale, but I'm going to scale it anyway.

45°

Hidden Hats

Middle, Rear, and Front are standing in line. An eccentric millionaire challenges them to a game. Choosing randomly from 3 white hats and 2 black hats, the millionaire will place a hat on each of the men. If a man guesses his hat color correctly, he receives one million dollars. If a man is wrong, he owes one million dollars. Rear, who can see two other hats, declines to give an answer. Middle, who can see one other hat, also declines to give an answer. Finally, Front, who cannot see any hats, states the color of his own hat? How?

The color of my hat is...

Jealous Husbands

Three couples need to cross a river but their boat only holds two people at a time. Furthermore, none of the men trust another man with his wife, so the men decide that no woman can be in the company of another man unless her husband is present. One of the couples crosses the river first. Deduce, without trial and error, who crosses the river on each of the remaining trips.

©1993 by Key Curriculum Press

Kisses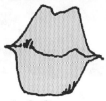

I f there are 100 people from Hollywood at a party and each kisses every other, how many kisses take place?

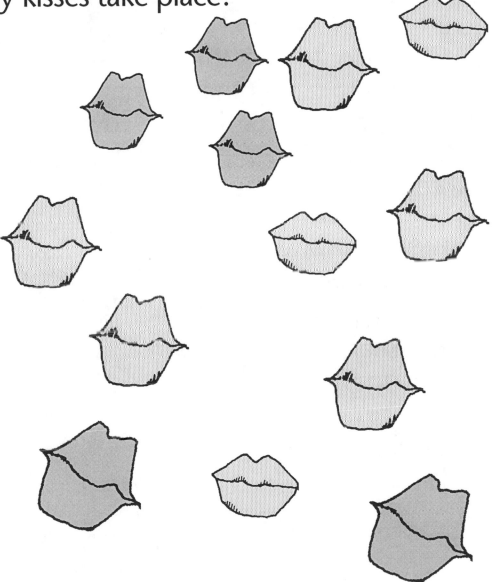

Let's Make a Deal

A game show contestant chooses one of three curtains, hoping that it is the one curtain with a brand new car behind it. A goat is behind each of the other two curtains. Monte Hall, the game show host, knows which curtain has the car behind it. Monte opens one of the non-chosen curtains, revealing a goat. He then gives the contestant the option of switching her choice. Oddly, the probability that the contestant will win depends on whether she changes her choice of curtains. Explain.

©1993 by Key Curriculum Press

Manhole Cover

Why are manholes and their covers circular?

Marble Race

If a bug sits within the tread of a bicycle tire while the tire rolls along the ground, the bug travels along a path known as a cycloid. Suppose that a marble is placed on one of the inclines of an inverted cycloid. Interestingly, this cycloid ramp will elicit a faster trip to the bottom than any other shape! Now suppose that a marble is placed on each of the two inclines of an inverted cycloid at unequal distances from the center. Intuitively, which marble will reach the bottom first if the marbles are released simultaneously?

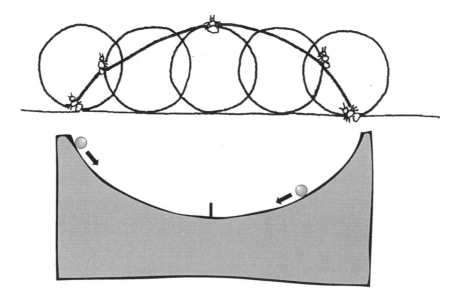

Miniature Golf

You wish to putt the ball so that it rebounds off both the 12 foot wall and the 24 foot wall into the hole. How far from the starting wall should the ball strike each side?

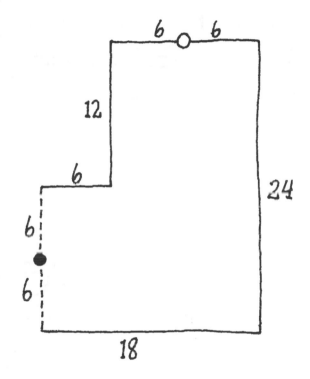

Necklace

You have four chains of three links each. How can you join them into one 12-link necklace (a closed loop) after cutting and joining only three links?

Nine Dots

Connect all nine dots with just four straight lines without lifting your pencil.

Opposing Views

Shown below are the front, left, and right views of an object. What does this object look like? For your answer, give a three dimensional sketch.

Front View

Left View

Right View

Paradox

Explain the contradiction between the first and last lines.

$$a = b + c, c \text{ does not equal } 0$$
$$(a - b)a = (a - b)(b + c)$$
$$a^2 - ab = ab + ac - b^2 - bc$$
$$a^2 - ab - ac = ab + ac - b^2 - bc - ac$$
$$a(a - b - c) = b(a - b - c)$$
$$a - b$$

Peanuts

A woman has some peanuts. She sees a friend at the door and she quickly eats a peanut before her friend enters and takes one half of the remaining peanuts. She sees another friend at the door and she quickly eats another peanut before the second friend enters and takes one half of the remaining peanuts. Finally, she sees a third friend at the door and she quickly eats another peanut before the third friend enters and takes one half of the remaining peanuts, leaving her with only one peanut. How many peanuts did the woman originally have?

Philosopher

One day at noon, Laura runs to the top of a mountain. She sits and ponders the meaning of life until the next day at noon at which time she runs down the mountain along the same trail that she ran up. Was she necessarily at some point on the mountain trail at the same time on both days? Prove your answer.

Photograph

A man looks at a photograph and says, "Brothers and sisters have I none, but that man's father is my father's son." The man himself is not in the photograph. Who is?

Polyhedra

A *regular polyhedron* is a solid whose faces are identical regular polygons meeting in each corner in exactly the same way. (A regular polygon has congruent sides and angles.) Only five such solids exist, and the number of faces, corners, and edges for each solid is shown at right. Find an equation that relates the number of faces, corners, and edges for each. (Interestingly, the same equation holds for any polyhedron.)

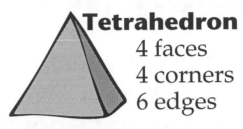

Tetrahedron
4 faces
4 corners
6 edges

Cube
6 faces
8 corners
12 edges

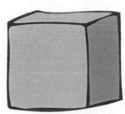

Octahedron
8 faces
6 corners
12 edges

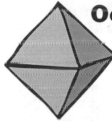

Dodecahedron
12 faces
20 corners
30 edges

Icosahedron
20 faces
12 corners
30 edges

Queens

Place 8 queens on a chessboard so that no two queens lie on the same row, column, or diagonal. Surprisingly, the solution is anything but symmetrical.

©1993 by Key Curriculum Press

Radius

What is the radius of the circle below?

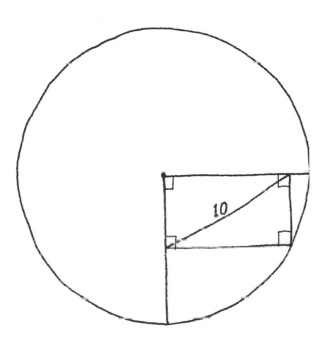

Sequence Time

What comes next?

-, E, '', |, ⊏, ''', ',

Soda

Sip and Gulp enter a bar and each orders a soda on ice. Gulp gulps down his drink while Sip sips his drink slowly. Some time later, Sip dies of poisoning. Both men were perfectly healthy before entering the bar and both received identical drinks. Why did only one die?

Squares

The figure below shows 15 identical squares that are stacked so that only 1 is entirely visible and the other 14 are partly visible. List the squares in order from top to bottom.

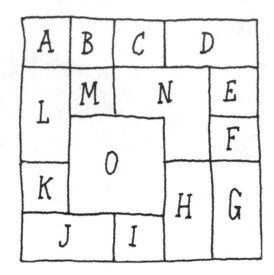

Stair Climber

Each morning a girl leaves her apartment on the twentieth floor, gets on the elevator, rides to the first floor, gets off the elevator, leaves the building, and goes to work. Each afternoon the girl returns from school, enters the building, gets on the elevator, rides to the tenth floor, gets off the elevator, climbs the stairs to the twentieth floor, and returns to her apartment. Why does she climb the last ten flights?

Swimmer

A two mile pier and a one mile pier extend perpendicularly into the ocean with four miles of shore between the two piers. A swimmer wishes to swim from the end of the longer pier to the end of the shorter pier with one rest stop on the beach. Assuming that the swimmer recalls that, in any right triangle, the hypotenuse^2 = leg^2 + leg^2, find the shortest possible swim.

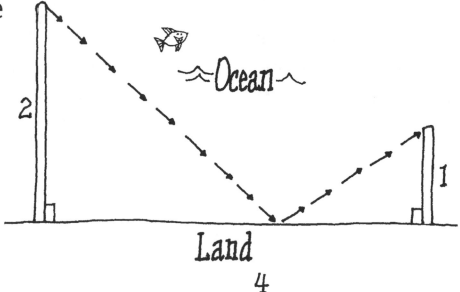

Three Circles

Draw three circles so that each dot is completely contained in its own region. The enclosure of each dot may consist of an arc from the original circle.

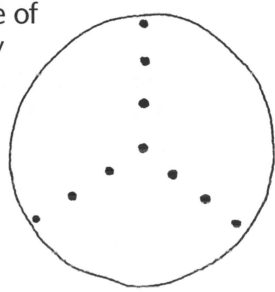

#45

Three Holes

A piece of plywood has three holes in it: a circular hole with a two-inch diameter, a square hole with a two-inch side, and a triangular hole with a two-inch base and height. Can you construct, draw, or describe just one object that completely plugs each hole AND passes completely through each hole?

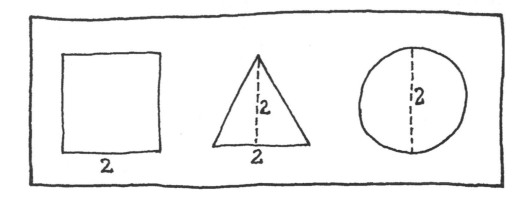

Two-Mile Drive

If one has already driven one mile at 30 mph, how fast must one drive the second mile so that the average speed for the trip equals 60 mph? (The answer is not 90 mph.)

Two Squares

Draw two squares so that each dot is completely contained in a region by itself. Each dot's surrounding enclosure may include segments of either the original square or new squares or both.

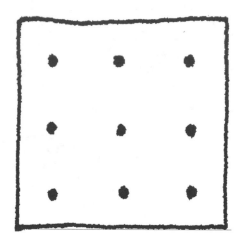

Water Jugs

An eight gallon jug is full and both a three gallon jug and a five gallon jug are empty. Without using any other containers, divide the water into two equal amounts.

What Comes Next?

st, nd, rd, th,

HINTS

1. Ant and Crumb

First Hint: "Unfold" the room into 2 dimensions. Note that there are three unfoldings that provide a surface for the line segment between the start and end points.

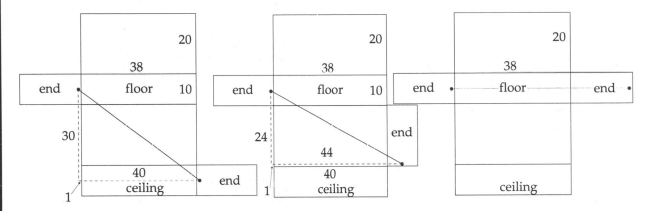

Second Hint: For each of the unfoldings, draw a right triangle. The hypotenuse connects the start and end points and the legs are parallel to the edges of the room.

2. Bike Pedal

Hint: The first answer is counter-clockwise (that is, the pedals rotate backward).

3. Birthdays

Hint: Perhaps you can begin by figuring out how many possible pairs exist between n people. As n increases: 2, 3, 4, ..., the number of matches increases quickly: 1, 3, 6, 10, 15, 21, 28, 36, 45. This realization will usually lead to a more reasonable estimate.

4. Bloodhound

Hint: How much time elapsed while the bloodhound ran?

5. Boat and Anchor

Hint: If the anchor were extremely heavy and the boat were very large and deep, what would happen to the boat?

6. Boys and Girls

Hint: The probability of an event

$$\frac{\text{number of possible outcomes in which the event occurs}}{\text{total number of } \textit{equiprobable} \text{ possible outcomes}}$$

7. Bugs On Bikes

Hint: Try drawing these two paths for two wheels of very different size.

8. Bumpy Road

Hint: The shape should have corners to fit into each crevice.

9. Cake

Hint: Imagine a cake, not a circle.

10. Census Taker

First Hint: Consider the sums of each set of three numbers that multiply to 36.
Second Hint: The leap year date of birth is misleading. However, note that only one son was born in a leap year.

11. Chaperone

Hint: More that one can return on the chair.

12. Counterfeit

Hint: You may want to reveal several beginning steps of the solution as a hint, as this problem is quite difficult.

13. Crying Wolf

Hint: An anagram has the same letters, rearranged. A homonym sounds the same. An antonym has the opposite meaning. If you get stuck trying to think of an antonym of foul, think baseball or weather.

14. Cyclic Number

Hint: Write out each of the five products and infer what numbers $a, b, c, d, e,$ and f cannot equal. By deduction and elimination, the solution can be found.

15. Date Dice

Hint: There is one digit that is not needed.

16. Dating Game

Hint: Bachelor 2 and Bachelor 3 contradict each other.

17. Dental Dilemma

Hint: For every 1001 people who are tested, consider how many test positive.

18. Dominoes

Hint: Consider the colors of any two adjacent checkerboard squares and the colors of opposite corner squares.

19. The Earth's Equator

Hint: The answer does not depend on the size of the Earth. In fact, if 100 feet were added to a string wrapped snugly around Jupiter's equator, the answer would not change.

20. Fork in the Road

Hint: When one lies about having lied, one has told the truth.

21. Four Weights

Hint: Begin by finding the integers that can be obtained with only two or three weights.

22. Helix

Hint: Let the ant's path be represented by the hypotenuse of a right triangle.

23. Hidden Hats

First Hint: First list all seven permutations of three black or white hats, but not three black hats.
Second Hint: Consider the orderings that are not possible given the responses of the first two men.

24. Jealous Husbands

Hint: There are two people in the boat on every trip over and on only one of the trips back.

25. Kisses

Hint: If 2 people, then 1 kiss; if 3 people, then 1 + 2 kisses; ... if 100 people, then $1 + 2 + 3 + ... + 98 + 99$ kisses. Can you think of a clever way to add $1 + 2 + 3 + ... + 98 + 99$ without actually entering each number into a calculator?

26. Let's Make a Deal

Hint: What is the probability that she wins without changing?

27. Manhole Cover

Hint: If a manhole were square, what might happen to its cover?

28. Marble Race

Hint: What advantage might the marble with the steep initial slope have over the other?

HINTS

29. Miniature Golf

Hint: The following diagram shows how one can deduce the point of impact for a one-bounce shot.

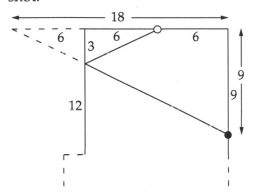

30. Necklace

Hint: Three of the four chains remain intact.

31. Nine Dots

Hint: The lines can be any length.

32. Opposing Views

Hint:

Top View

33. Paradox

Hint: Consider the quantity $a - b - c$.

34. Peanuts

Hint: Work backwards.

35. Philosopher

Hint: Imagine that.Laura's twin begins climbing the mountain at noon on the second day.

36. Photograph

Hint: Who is his father's son?

37. Polyhedra

Hint: The equation involves only the operation of addition.

38. Queens

Hint: It can be done with or without a queen in one of the corners.

39. Radius

Hint: One cannot and need not deduce the length and width of the rectangle.

40. Sequence Time

Hint: Think digital.

41. Soda

Hint: Consider their drinks over the course of time.

42. Squares

Hint: Begin by removing the top square and then either visualize or draw the remaining squares after removing each square.

43. Stair Climber

Hint: Consider the arrangements of the elevator buttons.

44. Swimmer

Hint: Suppose the one-mile pier extended inland rather than into the ocean.

45. Three Circles

Hint: The circles overlap and are equal in size.

46. Three Holes

Hint: First try to find a shape that can fit into both the square and the circle, and then remember that there are three dimensions, or perspectives.

47. Two-Mile Drive

Hint: Consider how much time elapsed during the first mile.

48. Two Squares

Hint: The squares differ in size.

49. Water Jugs

Hint: Never pour contents of one container into another unless at least one is either empty or full; otherwise, you are reversing your progress.

50. What Comes Next?

Hint: Pay attention to the first item.

ANSWERS

1. Ant and Crumb

Answer: 50 feet. The two legs have lengths 30 and 40. The hypotenuse equals the square root of the sum of the legs squared, or 50. (See figure in Hints section.)

2. Bike Pedal

Answer:
1. counter-clockwise
2. backward
3. backward
Try it.

3. Birthdays

Answer: 23

Intuitive Solution:

Note that there is 1 possible match in a group of two people, $1 + 2 = 3$ possible matches in a group of three people, $1 + 2 + 3 = 6$ possible matches in a group of four people, etc. This sequence of numbers grows quite quickly and reaches 253 after 23 people. Thus, the possibility of a match is much greater than most would guess.

Exact Solution:

P(no match within group of 2) = 364/365

P(no match within group of 3) = (364/365)(363/365)

P(no match within group of 4) = (364/365)(363/365)(362/365)

P(no match within group of 23) = (364/365)(363/365)(362/365) ... (343/365) = .49.

Therefore, P(match within group of 23) = 1– .49 = 51% chance of a match.

4. Bloodhound

Answer: 100 miles. The guard will catch the prisoner in 10 hours. Therefore, the dog will also run for 10 hours at a pace of 10 mph.

5. Boat and Anchor

Answer: The water level falls. The boat with the anchor will displace much more water than the anchor by itself.

6. Boys and Girls

Answer: Of four possible permutations, Tanya's children are either boy-boy, boy-girl, or girl-boy, giving a 1 in 3, or 1/3, chance of two boys. Bill's children are either boy-boy or boy-girl, giving a 1 in 2, or 1/2, chance of two boys.

7. Bugs on Bikes

Answer: The bugs travel an equal distance.

8. Bumpy Road

Answer: Square.

9. Cake

Answer:

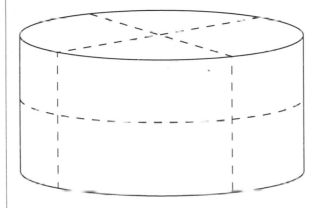

10. Census Taker

Answer: Their ages are 2, 2, and 9. The children are either 1-1-36, 1-2-18, 1-3-12, 1-4-9, 1-6-6, 2-2-9, 2-3-6, or 3-3-4. Of these eight combinations, all but two add to unique totals. If the address of the house next door had equaled one of these totals, the man would not have returned. Therefore, the ages are either 1-66 or 2-2-9, both of which add to 13. If the children had been 1-6-6, there would be no oldest son.

ANSWERS

11. Chaperone

Answer: The counselor and Alice cross over, the counselor returns, the counselor and one of the brats cross over, the counselor and Alice return, the counselor and the other brat cross over, the counselor returns, and the counselor and Alice cross over.

12. Counterfeit

Answer: Compare 1-2-3-4 and 5-6-7-8.
If 1-2-3-4 > 5-6-7-8, compare 1-6-7 and 2-5-12.
   If 1-6-7 > 2-5-12, compare 1 and 4.
      If 1 > 4, then 1 is heavy.
      If 1 = 4, then 5 is light.
   If 1-6-7 = 2-5-12, compare 3 and 4.
      If 3 > 4, then 3 is heavy.
      If 3 = 4, then 8 is light.
      If 3 < 4, then 4 is heavy.
   If 1-6-7 < 2-5-l2, compare 6 and 7.
      If 6 > 7, then 7 is light.
      If 6 = 7, then 2 is heavy.
      If 6 < 7, then 6 is light.
If l-2-3-4 = 5-6-7-8, compare l-2-3 and 9-10-11.
   If 1-2-3 > 9-10-11, compare 9 and 11.
      If 9 > 11, then 11 is light.
      If 9 = 11, then 10 is light.
      If 9 < 11, then 9 is light.
   If 1-2-3 = 9-10-11, compare 10 and 12.
      If 10 > 12, then 12 is light.
      If 10 < 12, then 12 is heavy.
   If 1-2-3 < 9-10-11, compare 9 and 11.
      If 9 > 11, then 9 is heavy.
      If 9 = 11, then 10 is heavy.
      If 9 < 11, then 11 is heavy.
If l-2-3-4 < 5-6-7-8, compare 2-3-5 and l-6-12.
   If 2-3-5 > 1-6-12, compare 5 and 8.
      If 5 > 8, then 5 is heavy.
      If 5 = 8, then 1 is light.
   If 2-3-5 = 1-6-12, compare 7 and 8.
      If 7 > 8, then 7 is heavy.
      If 7 = 8, then 4 is light.
      If 7 < 8, then 8 is heavy.
   If 2-3-5 < 1-6-12, compare 2 and 3.
      If 2 > 3, then 3 is light.
      If 2 = 3, then 6 is heavy.
      If 2 < 3, then 2 is light.

13. Crying Wolf

Answer: Fear.

14. Cyclic Number

Answer: 142857. This is the only number known to have this cyclic property.

15. Date Dice

Answer: 0,1,2,6,7,8 and 0,1,2,3,4,5. The 6 can be turned upside down to represent the 9.

16. Dating Game

Answer: Bachelor 1. Since Bachelor 2 and Bachelor 3 contradict each other, one of them must be telling the truth. Since either Bachelor 1 or Bachelor 2 is the only truth teller, Bachelor 1 must be a liar. Therefore, Bachelor 1 is the tallest.

17. Dental Dilemma

Answer: 20%. For every 1001 tested, 1 has the condition. That person will test positive. Of the remaining 1000, 4 test falsely positive. Therefore, of those that test positive, only 1 in 5 actually have the condition.

18. Dominoes

Answer: Any two adjacent squares of a checkerboard will be different in color. Therefore, each domino must cover a square of each color. But the two missing squares have the same color, leaving only 30 squares with that color, not 31 as required.

19. The Earth's Equator

Answer: Since $C = 2\pi r$, then $r = C/2\pi$. Thus, if the circumference increases by 100 feet, the radius increases by 100 ft$/2\pi$, or about 32 feet, which is high enough to drive a Mack truck underneath.

20. Fork in the Road

Answer: "If I were to ask you if the left fork led to my destination, what would you say?"

ANSWERS

21. Four Weights

Answer: 1, 3, 9, 27. Incredibly, these powers of three combine so that no object weighing between 1 and 40, inclusive, can be weighed in more than one way.

22. Helix

Answer: Consider the 45-45-90 right triangle shown below, where the hypotenuse equals the ant's walking distance and the height equals 6 inches, the height of the can. Because both legs of this right triangle are equal in length, the hypotenuse must equal $6\sqrt{2}$ inches, or about 8.49 inches.

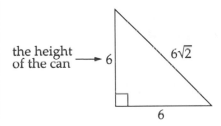

the height of the can → 6

$6\sqrt{2}$

6

23. Hidden Hats

Answer: White. Rear, Middle, and Front are wearing, respectively, either WWW, WWB, WBW, WBB, BWW, BWB, or BBW. Eliminate WBB, for if Rear had seen two black hats, he would have known that his hat was white. Eliminate BWB and WWB, for if Middle had seen a black hat on Front, he would have known that his hat was white. Of the remaining 4 possibilities, Front is always wearing a white hat.

24. Jealous Husbands

Answer: One couple over, the one man back, the two women over, any one woman back, the two wifeless men over, either couple back, the two men over, the one woman back, any two women over, the one wifeless man back, the last couple over.

25. Kisses

Answer: 4950. $1 + 2 + 3 + ... + 99 = (1 + 99) + (2 + 98) + (3 + 97) + ... + (48 + 52) + (49 + 51) + 50 = 49(100) + 50 = 4950$

26. Let's Make A Deal

Answer: If she does not switch, she has a 1/3 chance of winning. Therefore, she must have a 2/3 chance of winning when she does switch. If this does not convince you, try it many times.

27. Manhole Cover

Answer: If manholes and their covers were anything but circular, the cover could fall through the hole.

28. Marble Race

Answer: The two marbles arrive simultaneously, regardless of where along the inclines the marbles are placed.

29. Miniature Golf

Answer: 3 feet and 9 feet, respectively.

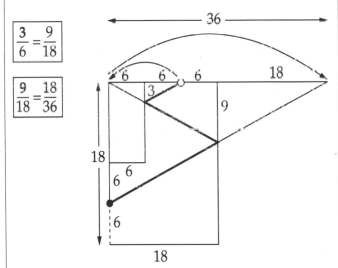

$$\frac{3}{6} = \frac{9}{18}$$

$$\frac{9}{18} = \frac{18}{36}$$

30. Necklace

Answer: Cut the three links from one chain and use each to join the remaining three chains into one loop.

ANSWERS

31. Nine Dots

Answer:

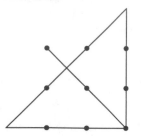

32. Opposing Views

Answer:

33. Paradox

Answer: Because $a - b - c = 0$, the last step involves division by zero.

34. Peanuts

Answer: 15. Working backwards, the woman had 1, 2, 3, 6, 7, 14, and then 15 peanuts.

35. Philosopher

Answer: Suppose that Laura's cosmic twin ran up the mountain exactly as Laura had, but exactly 24 hours later. With Laura running down the mountain, the two would have to meet.

36. Photograph

Answer: His son.

37. Polyhedra

Answer: Faces + corners = edges + 2.

38. Queens

Answer: (4,1); (7,2); (1,3); (8,4); (5,5); (2,6); (6,7); (3,8) or (6,1); (3,2); (5,3); (7,4); (1,5); (4,6); (2,7); (8,8).

39. Radius

Answer: 10.

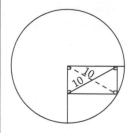

40. Sequence Time

Answer:

41. Soda

Answer: The ice, which was poisoned, started to melt before Sip was finished.

42. Squares

Answer: ONMLKJIHGFEDCBA

43. Stair Climber

Answer: The girl could reach the elevator button for the first floor, but was too short to reach the button for the twentieth floor.

ANSWERS

44. Swimmer

Answer: 5 miles. Suppose that the swimmer swims to the coast and then has a choice of whether to swim to the end of the ocean pier or "swim" to the end of an imaginary 1-mile pier that extends inland. Notice that the minimal distance is unaffected by the choice. Therefore, simply draw a line between the ends of the 2-mile pier and the imaginary 1 mile pier. That line is the hypotenuse of a right triangle with legs of length 3 and 4.

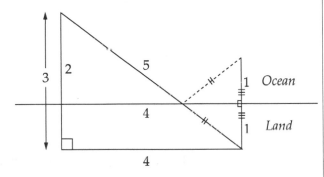

45. Three Circles

Answer:

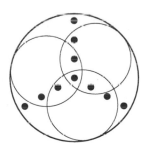

46. Three Holes

Answer:

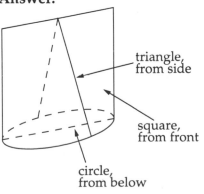

47. Two-Mile Drive

Answer: Impossible. 2 minutes have already elapsed during the first mile, but a two-mile trip must be completed in 2 minutes for an average of 60 mph.

48. Two Squares

Answer:

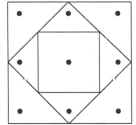

49. Water Jugs

Answer: Jugs 3-5-8 have the following amounts between each pouring:
0-0-8, 0-5-3, 3-2-3, 0-2-6, 2-0-6, 2-5-1, 3-4-1, 0-4-4.

50. What Comes Next?

Answer: th. 1st, 2nd, 3rd, 4th, 5th.